Nature

NOTES

Canadian representatives: General Publishing Co., Ltd.,
30 Lesmill Road, Don Mills, Ontario M3B 2T6.

ISBN 1–56138–484–4

Cover design by Toby Schmidt
Interior design by Lili Schwartz
Cover and interior illustrations by Valerie Coursen
Typography by Deborah Lugar
Printed in the United States

This book may be ordered by mail from the publisher.
Please add $1.00 for postage and handling.
But try your bookstore first!

Running Press Book Publishers
125 South Twenty-second Street
Philadelphia, Pennsylvania 19103–4399

Nature
N O T E S

Running Press
Philadelphia • London

*B*eauty is built into every jot and tittle of creation—into
every atomic brick! Beauty soaks reality like water
fills a rag.

Chet Raymo
20th-century American writer

I should like to enjoy this summer

flower by flower. . . .

André Gide (1869–1951)
French writer

Nature is not a competition. It doesn't really matter, when you go out, if you don't identify anything. What matters is the feeling heart.

Richard Adams, b. 1920
English writer

The field has eyes, the wood has ears; I will look, be silent, and listen.

HIERONYMUS BOSCH (1450-1516)
FLEMISH ARTIST

Only the mountain has lived long

enough to listen objectively

to the howl of a wolf.

Aldo Leopold (1888–1948)
American conservationist

It is only the . . . shortness of human life that gives each individual a sense of the permanence of his background. The land we all walk upon has been under the sea many times, and it will be submerged again.

JACQUETTA HAWKES, B. 1910
BRITISH ARCHAEOLOGIST

No plant, no land or sea, no part of

any land or sea is here forever.

Wherever we stand, we are

only stewards.

Frank Herbert (1920–1986)
American writer

It seems to me that we all look at

Nature too much, and live

with her too little.

Oscar Wilde (1854–1900)
Irish poet and playwright

. . . the raw experience of nature . . . pours into the unconscious, the world of dreams, the source of myth.

Diane Ackerman, b. 1948
American writer and poet

Love of nature counts much for sanity

in later life.

ANNA BOTSFORD COMSTOCK (1854–1930)
AMERICAN SCIENTIST

*If I wanted to contemplate what is to me the deepest of all mysteries,
I should choose as my object lesson a snowflake under a lens and an
amoeba under a microscope.*

Joseph Wood Crutch (1893–1970)
American writer

I know of no sculpture, painting or music that exceeds the compelling spiritual commands of the soaring shape of granite cliff and dome, of patina of light on rock and forest, and of the thunder and whispering of the falling, flowing waters.

Ansel Adams (1902–1984)
American photographer

Nature is visible thought.

HEINRICH HEINE (1797–1856)
GERMAN POET

We like to think of nature as unerring. In reality, everything
it does is an approximate mistake. Its every calculation is
short-term, a quick fix.

Richard Powers, b. 1957
American writer

Nature is everywhere familiar in macrocosm and microcosm, in the dip and resurgence of the night-sky constellations and in the shower of green leaves welling up around old dead seed stalks.

ROBERT FINCH
20TH-CENTURY AMERICAN EDITOR

Deep in the greens of summer sing the

lives I've come to love.

Theodore Roethke, b. 1908
American poet

With the rising of the sun in the cool
morning, a fresh day presented itself . . .
a fresh day was a gift that might produce
any manner of wonders.

LARRY MCMURTRY, B. 1936
AMERICAN WRITER

These great brown hills move in herds, humped like bison before the traveling eye. Massive above the farms, they file and hulk daylong across every distance; and bending come as the sun sinks orange and small beyond their heavy shoulders, shaggy at evening, to drink among the shadowy lakes.

Robert Wallace, b. 1919
American writer

Wind moving through grass so that the grass quivers. This moves me with an emotion I don't even understand.

Katherine Mansfield (1888–1923)
New Zealand-born English writer

The sky was without cloud,
washed pure by the previous
night's storm and of a deliciously
tender and ethereal blue; the air as
sharp as lemon-juice, yet as
clean and cleansing.

John Fowles, b. 1926
American writer

$\mathcal{S}$o little lies between you and the sky.

So little lies between you and the earth.

Leslie Marmon Silko, b. 1948
American writer

One seems to have more sky than earth

in one's world.

GEORGIA O'KEEFE (1887–1986)
AMERICAN ARTIST

Junipers in the mountains were thickly hung with berries, and the air was unadulterated gin.

John McPhee, b. 1931
American writer

I come into the presence of still water. And I feel above me the day-blind stars waiting with their light. For a time, I rest in the grace of the world, and am free.

Wendell Berry, b. 1934
American poet

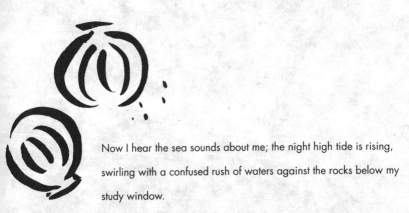

Now I hear the sea sounds about me; the night high tide is rising,

swirling with a confused rush of waters against the rocks below my

study window.

RACHEL CARSON (1907–1964)
AMERICAN BIOLOGIST

*The earth is built upon crystals; the
granite rock is only a denser and more
compact snow, or a kind of ice that was
vapor once and may be vapor again.*

John Burroughs (1837–1921)
American naturalist

The world is big but it is comprehensible.

R. BUCKMINSTER FULLER (1895-1983)
AMERICAN ARCHITECT

The most incomprehensible thing

about the universe is that it is

comprehensible.

Albert Einstein (1879–1955)
German-born American physicist

Nature is always hinting at us. It hints over and over again.

And suddenly we take the hint.

ROBERT FROST (1874–1963)
AMERICAN POET

Birth, life, and death—each took place on the hidden side of a leaf.

Toni Morrison, b. 1931
American writer

In nature there are neither rewards nor

punishments—only consequences.

ROBERT G. INGERSOLL (1833–1899)
AMERICAN LAWYER AND ORATOR

Ethereal
Earth body moving
Delicate robust petals opening
Sweet pollen bubbling from
Elegant strong stamens
Exuberant spring bud
Jewel
Balancing
Above
Sinuous
Stem
Slender leaves extend
Gathering
Giving
Breezes nestle
Storms challenge
Roots reach
Nourishing support
Annexing eternal gifts

Our purpose is to consciously, deliberately evolve toward a wiser, more liberated and luminous state of being; to return to Eden, make friends with the snake and set up our computers among the wild apple trees.

TOM ROBBINS, B. 1936
AMERICAN WRITER

*J*oy is drunk by all God's creatures

From the earth's abundant breast,

Good and bad, all things are nature's,

And with blameless joy are blessed.

Johann von Schiller (1759–1805)
German poet

All nature wears one universal grin.